Elder Cleop~ ~~~~ ~ ~~~~

Published by
Sebastian Press
Western American Diocese of the Serbian Orthodox Church

Edited by
Bishop Maxim (Vasiljević)

Prepress & printing
Interklima-grafika, Vrnjacka Banja, Serbia
Christian inspiration for youth series ; no. 5.
Copyright © 2018 Sebastian Press

Address all correspondence to:
Sebastian Press
1621 West Garvey Avenue
Alhambra, California 91803

Email: westsrbdio@gmail.com ❖ Website: http://www.westsrbdio.org

Names: Ilie, Cleopa, author. | Mănăstirea Sihăstria, illustrator. | Suvak, Diana, translator.

Title: Elder Cleopa stories for children. Volume 2 / illustrated by Monastery Sihastria, Romania ; translated by Diana Suvak.

Description: Alhambra, California : Sebastian Press / Western American Diocese of the Serbian Orthodox Church, [2018] | Series: Christian inspiration for youth series ; no. 5. | Includes bibliographical references. | Contents: Widow Anastasia's church -- A miracle with the Holy Cross.

Identifiers: ISBN: 978-1-936773-40-4

Subjects: LCSH: Orthodox Eastern Church--Doctrines--Juvenile literature. | Humility--Religious aspects --Orthodox Eastern Church--Juvenile literature. | Holy Cross--Juvenile literature. | Miracles-- Juvenile literature. | Christian literature for children. | Spiritual life--Christianity--Juvenile literature. | CYAC: Humility. | Holy Cross. | Miracles. | Christian life.

Classification:
LCC: BX384.Y68 I44 v.2 | DDC: 248.4/81909282--dc23

Elder Cleopa Stories for Children

Vol 2

Illustrated by
Monastery Sihastria, Romania

Sebastian Press 2018

Widow Anastasia's Church

Almost a thousand years ago, the emperor Nike-phoros Botaneiates of Constantinople (1078-1081) built a huge cathedral, almost as big as Saint Sophia. The consecration of the church was announced several months in advance, so that people would have time to come, since there were no cars, planes, or trains at that time.

All the carts were pulled by oxen, horses, and donkeys, and this is how everyone traveled. People needed several months to come if they lived far away. They needed to take food for the horses and the oxen. Therefore, when the consecration of the church was announced, a large spot was prepared in front of it, where many people could gather.

Patriarchs, 40 metropolitans, and thousands of priests came to the consecration of emperor Nike-phoros's church, because it was a royal church. The patriarchs of Jerusalem, Constantinople, and Alexandria came, as it was customary when a royal church was going to be consecrated.

Thousands of carts started to arrive for the feast of consecration. Some people brought rugs, while others brought barrels of wine or oil; some people brought flour, while others brought candles. Everyone brought what they could.

At that time, a 93-year-old woman named Anastasia lived in Constantinople. She had been a widow for 50 years and she always went to church and prayed to God. She lived on the outskirts of the town, next to the road where carts had to pass in order to go to the consecration. But she was extremely poor. She lived in a shack, and she didn't have any money. She didn't have oil, flour, or anything else to bring. She only had a sickle and a distaff.

She was a poor widow in terms of material possessions, but she was rich in terms of faith. In the winter she would spin hemp and wool, while in the summer she took her sickle and went into the wheat fields, helping people harvest or gathering ears of wheat that were left after people were done harvesting. She used to put the ears on a cloth, pound them, and make wheat. Thus, little by little, she filled up a sack of wheat for herself. This is how poor the widow Anastasia was!

As she watched oxen passing by pulling so many carts, which were filled with heavy burdens and food for the feast of consecration, the poor woman noticed that some of them only carried hay, so she thought to herself: "I don't have any money, I don't have any carpets, I don't have any oil, I don't have

anything. I'll just bring an armful of grass." So she grabbed her sickle and a small rope, but she didn't own any land that she could cut grass from. So how could she get some grass without causing anyone harm? She went to the very edge of someone's field, where she found some agropyron, a type of grass that is harmful to the harvest.

And the old woman cut one or two armfuls of grass, put the pile into a sack, and went to church.

Thousands and thousands of carts and oxen, which had come with barrels of oil and flour, were gathered there.

Then she noticed a couple of oxen that had finished eating their food. They had nothing left and were looking all around; they would have eaten more, but there was nothing left for them to eat.

Old Anastasia untied her sack of grass, put it in front of the oxen, and said: "Lord, please receive this armful of grass because I don't have anything else to bring for the consecration of this church; and please forgive me, for it didn't even come from my own field." And after she gave the grass to the oxen, she went to church weeping.

When she saw so many people and so many treasures ready to be sanctified – since the church had been adorned like a bride for her wedding – Anastasia went to the icons in the back, where women usually bow and pray. Old, poor, with a wrinkled face and an old scarf on her head, wearing some peasant shoes and an old skirt, she kneeled and prayed to the Lord:

– Lord, please forgive me, for I haven't brought any gifts to this church! I don't have anything. The emperor is emperor on earth and will also be emperor in heaven! But I, the wretched one, didn't have any money, didn't have anything...

And she was praying with tears.

And the emperor Nikephoros Botaneiates, together with his counsellors, imperial guards, soldiers, and the entire imperial retinue, also arrived there. The emperor's golden crown was shining like rays of sun on his head and he was wearing a royal mantle.

The scaffolding had already been taken away. Before entering the church, the emperor's counsellor, whose name was Peter, pointed to the inscrip-

tion above the door: "Your highness, look, do you like the inscription?" As you have probably seen in many churches, monasteries, and historical monuments, there is often an inscription above the door that says who built them.

There was a big marble board, on which it was written with golden letters: "To the glory of the Most Holy Trinity, of the Father, and of the Son, and of the Holy Spirit, I, the emperor Nikephoros Botaneiates, have built this holy church at my own expense." And the counsellor showed it to the emperor: "Do you like it?"

"Very much." He really liked the inscription.

And the emperor, accompanied by a multitude of generals, entered the church to see how it had been prepared for the consecration, which was going to take place the following day. They saw beautiful paintings, icons made of gold, beautiful curtains, golden vestments, chandeliers, tabernacles, chalices on the Holy Table, the Gospel, and everything that was needed.

Old Anastasia, who had brought an armful of grass, was also there and was weeping in front of the icons.

In the meantime, the angel of the Lord changed the emperor's inscription. It was written even more beautifully, with golden letters: "To the glory of the Most Holy Trinity, of the Father, and of the

Son, and of the Holy Spirit, I, the widow Anastasia, have built this holy church at my own expense."
    People started to read:

– Hey, what does it say there?

– What does it say?

– Well, look, it says that a widow built the church.

– But when the emperor went inside, his name was there.

– What if the emperor heard about this!

The scaffolding had been taken away, so no one could say that somebody could have made any changes.

– But it was only a few moments ago that the emperor entered the church and the inscription was read to him. Who could have changed the letters so quickly? This is a great miracle!

The people were afraid to tell the emperor, so they went to Peter, who was his counsellor and minister of internal affairs:

– Look, a great miracle has happened! We were entering the church and here's what the inscription said!

– Let's see. Oh, yes, you are right, this is a great miracle! Let me call the emperor! Your highness, come to the narthex for a moment!

The emperor always listened to him, for he was his trusted counsellor.

He went there. When he looked, he was astonished.

– But when we entered the church, the inscription mentioned my name!

– I know it was your name, your highness! Everybody knows this. But look what it says now!

– Woe to me, the sinner! This is a great miracle! Nobody but God could have done this. A great miracle indeed! I lost the church because I built it pridefully! He gave it to a widow!

He gathered his counsellors and told them the following:

– This church will not be consecrated until we find this widow! And when we find her, we will consecrate the church in her name, because God gave it to her, because she is greater before God than I am.

He commanded his people to search the entire kingdom and find widow Anastasia's address.

But God, wanting to reveal this quickly, revealed Anastasia through another widow, who was about the same age as her and who was present there among the people.

– Who are you asking about?

– A widow, Anastasia, whom the emperor is looking for.

– I know Anastasia! She lives there, on the outskirts of the town.

– What did you say? Come to the emperor!

She told the emperor where he could find widow Anastasia, so he sent some messengers to look for her and bring her to church.

He sent over three generals who were riding their horses, because there were no cars at that time.

– Hurry and bring her here, but don't frighten her. Tell her that, for the feast of consecration, I will give a cow to each widow, so that she won't be afraid.

The messengers, riding their horses, went quickly to the outskirts of Constantinople to look for Anastasia and to bring her to the emperor.

There, they saw some children playing ring toss.

– Hey, children, do you know where old Anastasia lives?

One of the older children said:

– Old Anastasia lives there, in the garden.

– Is she at home?

– No, she's not at home, she went to the fair with an armful of grass.

The children didn't know about the consecration of the church. They thought that was a fair.

– First, let's confirm that she's not at home.

And they went to the widow's house walking on a stile. When they arrived at her door, guess what they saw! There were no locks or bolts! For the person who doesn't own anything is not afraid of anything. They only saw two metal rings tied around with hemp thread and a stick leaning against the door.

This was a sign that the old woman was not at home. Those were the locks she had. There was

nothing to steal from her. She was gone to the consecration of the church.

Then, the three generals who had been sent by the emperor as messengers turned their horses and came to report to the emperor.

– Your highness, we went there. She has a small house on the outskirts of Constantinople. Some children were playing there and said that old Anastasia went to church with an armful of grass and that she's somewhere around here, among the people.

Then the emperor said:

– Woe to me; it would be such a miracle if we could find her!

The widow who had told them where Anastasia lived gathered another 10 to 15 women who knew her and said: "Let's look for Anastasia, because the emperor is calling her." And they went inside the church, walking among the people. One of them said: "Anastasia is praying there, in front of the icons."

Then they went to the emperor.

– Anastasia is inside the church, she is praying to the Savior!– If she's inside the church, bring her to me, but tell her not to be afraid, for she has never seen me. Send some old women and tell her that, for the feast of consecration, the emperor gives a cow to every old person.

So they went to the poor old woman. She was full of tears, praying in front of the Savior's icon.

They called her:

– Anastasia, come here.

The poor woman was wiping her tears.

– Anastasia, come, the emperor has called us.

– Oh my goodness, I'm afraid!

– Don't be. He is calling all the widows because he wants to give them a cow.

They told her this so that she wouldn't be afraid. And when she heard that they would give her a cow, she said:

– Let's go, although I have never faced the emperor in my entire life.

About 30 widows were gathered there and they went to the emperor.

The emperor was waiting together with the generals and his royal retinue. When the widows went there, they all stood before him. And Anastasia was standing in the middle. The emperor was sitting down, wearing a golden crown on his head, and was surrounded by the empress, the generals, and the country's flags.

One man said to him:

– Do you see that short woman standing in the middle and looking down? That's Anastasia.

Then, the emperor stood up from his chair, took his golden crown, kneeled, and put his crown next to Anastasia's feet. She was almost paralyzed with fear, but the emperor said to her:

– Don't be afraid, mother! What is your name?

– Anastasia.

– Don't be afraid, Anastasia, for you have made yourself worthy of tremendous grace from God. What gift did you bring this morning for the consecration of this church?

– I didn't bring any gifts, your highness, because I'm poor.

She didn't believe that the grass she gave to the oxen was a gift.

– Anastasia, you must have brought something. You brought an armful of grass and thus you took away my church!

– Yes, I brought some grass, but I didn't think of it as a gift because I cut it from someone else's field.

She didn't think the gift was from her.

– Anastasia, your armful of grass was more valuable in God's eyes than all the billions of silver and gold that I spent on this cathedral.

She was afraid that she would be punished.

– Look, this royal church that I spent so many golden coins on was built exclusively at my own expense and now the inscription says that it was built by Anastasia!

And the emperor said:

– The other widows should bring this woman outside and take good care of her, for she is like my mother. I'm happy that I found her.

They went outside and they asked one of the servants to read the inscription. She was only listening, because she couldn't read.

– Listen to what this says, Anastasia!

And it was written thus: "To the glory of the Most Holy Trinity, of the Father, and of the Son, and of the Holy Spirit, I, the widow Anastasia, have built this holy church at my own expense."

– Is this your name?

– Yes, but I didn't write that.

She was afraid that she would be blamed for it.

– I didn't write that because I can't write.

– Don't be afraid, mother Anastasia, for it was God who wrote that. You didn't write it, it was the angel of God who did. Your armful of grass was more valuable than all the treasures that I gave to this church. Look, God gave you the church and it will be yours forever.

The poor woman was astonished. Everyone was amazed: "This is such a great miracle!" And the next day they consecrated the church in her name, the Church of Saint Anastasia.

And when the blessed Anastasia of Constantinople passed away, the emperor built her grave in the Holy Altar: "Here, inside the church that God miraculously gave to her, rests the widow Anastasia."

Here's what I want to tell you: Do you see how valuable an armful of grass brought with faith to some hungry oxen can be? Do you see how precious it was in God's eyes? More precious than all the emperor's treasures. It was precious because the poor woman brought it with humility, for she had nothing else to bring. This is what I want to tell you about almsgiving: Even if you can't give much, give what you can. Even if you give only one potato to a needy person, that's very good. You see, when you're really hungry, even one potato is good. This is how you must think: Even if you don't give much, when you give something and you're sorry for not giving more, at that moment almsgiving and humility are joined together and reach God immediately.

Saint Ephrem the Syrian says: "God does not look at how much you have given, but how willingly you have given it." No matter how small your gift is, if you give it with humility and sadness for not being able to do more, that's what real almsgiving is.

A Miracle with the Holy Cross

In the east there is a very big country called India, which is inhabited by many people and is full of all sorts of treasures and crops. It is richer than other countries, surrounded by water and located close to the borders of China. This country was enlightened at some point by the Holy Apostle Thomas, but it didn't completely abandon idolatry because many people were hardhearted and didn't want to receive the teaching of salvation.

In that country, some of our Christian missionaries have preached the Gospel with great zeal. In one village, a poor missionary succeeded in converting to Christianity several Hindu families who had been worshiping the god Brahma Krishna. And because those families converted to Christianity, the missionary built a big wooden cross in that village, which had the Savior in real size on it, and he decorated it nicely.

Those who believed in Christ bowed before the crucified Savior and the holy wooden cross. But the many other inhabitants turned with hatred against the few Christians and they beat and killed them, thus martyring them for believing in Christ.

Moreover, they went to the holy wooden cross
that had the crucified Christ on it and they started
to mock and to spit on the Savior, beating Him
with their sticks and smearing dirt on His cross.

And when they were in the middle of their mock-
ery, the crucified Savior turned His face to the right,
toward them, and said: "Why are you mocking Me?"

When they saw that the One they were spitting on turned towards them like a living person and asked them why they were mocking Him, some of

them were paralyzed with fear, while others ran to their teachers and said:

– Come and see a miracle! We were mocking Christ and we saw with our own eyes how He turned His face and said to us: "Why are you mocking Me?"

And they all went to the cross. When their teachers saw that Christ had turned His face, they became frightened; and they were all baptized, and all the inhabitants of that land were greatly shaken. In the place of that holy wooden cross, today there is a great cathedral. The cross with the crucified Savior Who turned His face is still located in the altar of that cathedral.

This is how the Savior reprimanded those who mocked Him, in order to make them repent.

Therefore, brothers, if this sign from the Cross of Christ was enough to paralyze some with fear, to turn others to repentance, and to awaken so many souls, what will happen when the Savior comes on heavenly clouds and when the Cross of Christ, brought with great glory by millions and millions of archangels and angels, shines millions of times brighter than the sun?

Content